Mel Bay Presents

Solo Pieces

for the

BEGINNING VIOLINIST

By Craig Duncan

1 2 3 4 5 6 7 8 9 0

Contents

		Violin	Piano
British Grenadiers		6	8
Caprice from Alceste	C. W. von Gluck	8	10
Fantasia	Georg Philipp Telemann	14	17
Gavotte	Arcangelo Corelli	11	14
Gavotte and Variation	Georg Friederic Handel	18	24
German Dance	Ludwig van Beethoven	13	16
The Harmonius Blacksmith	Georg Friederic Handel	9	12
Marche from Anna Magdalena's Notebook	Philipp Emanuel Bach	16	20
Menuet from Anna Magdalena's Notebook	Johann Sebastian Bach	17	22
Minuet	Georg Philipp Telemann	10	13
Ride, Ride	Dmitri Kabalevsky	12	15
Rigaudon	Henry Purcell	5	6
Rondo	Jean Francois Dandrieu	20	27
Surprise Symphony	Joseph Haydn	7	9
Two Hungarian Folk Tunes Bela Bartok	1. Allegro	3	4
	2. Scherzando	4	5
Waltz from the A Major Sonata	Wolfgang A. Mozart	15	18

Two Hungarian Folk Tunes

1. Allegro

Bela Bartok

2. Scherzando

Bela Bartok

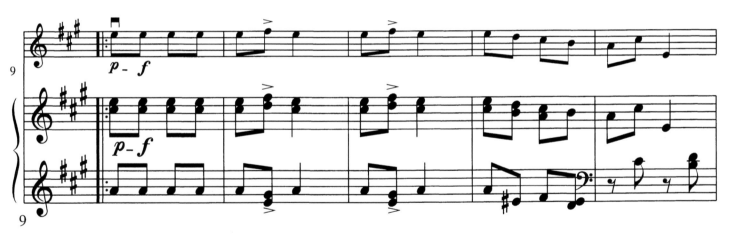

Rigaudon

Henry Purcell

British Grenadiers

Surprise Symphony

Joseph Haydn

Caprice from Alceste

C. W. von Gluck

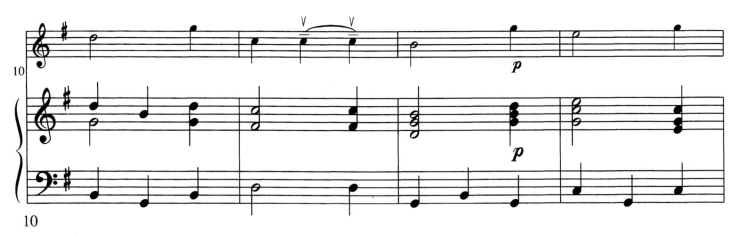

The Harmonius Blacksmith

George Friederic Handel

Minuet

Georg Philipp Telemann

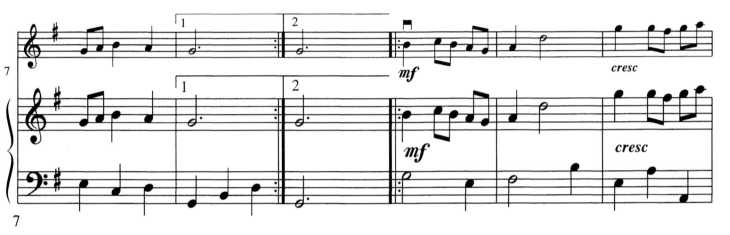

Gavotte

Arcangelo Corelli

Ride, Ride

Dmitri Kabalevsky

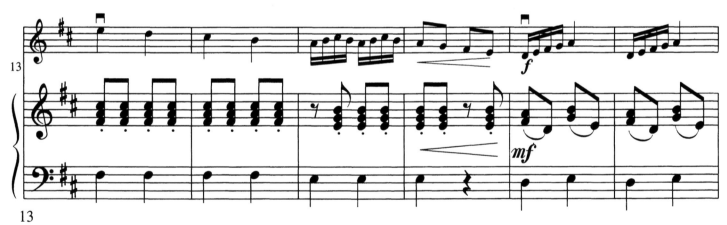

German Dance

Ludwig van Beethoven

Fantasia

Georg Philipp Telemann

Waltz
from the A major Sonata

Wolfgang A. Mozart

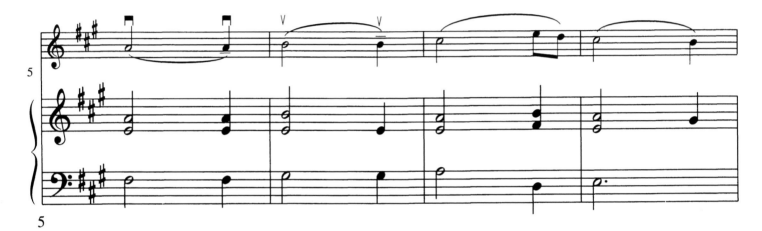

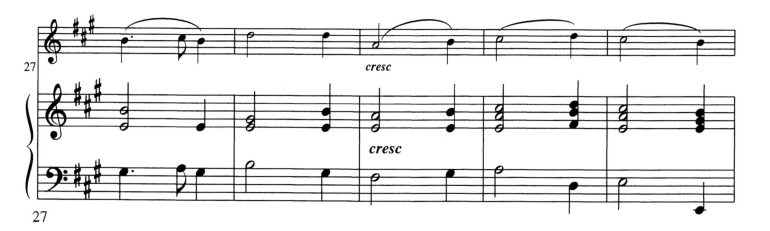

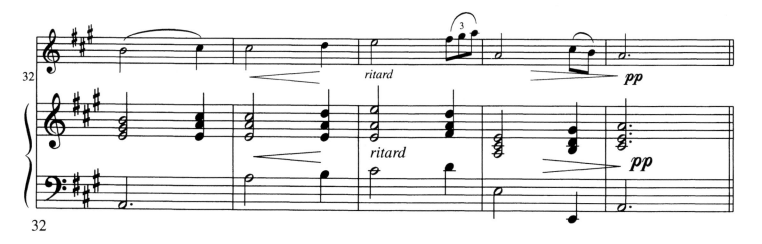

Marche

Philipp Emanuel Bach

Menuet
from Anna Magdalena's Notebook

J. S. Bach

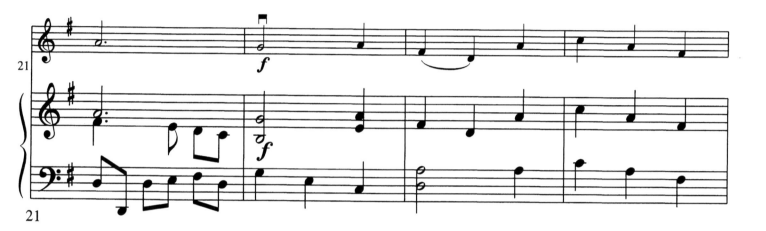

Gavotte and Variation

Georg Friederic Handel

34

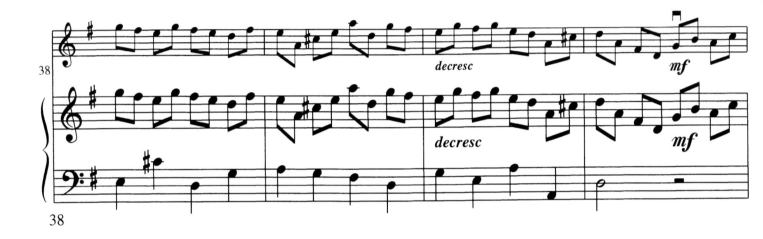

38

42

46

Rondo

Jean Francois Dandrieu